Days Off

Days Off

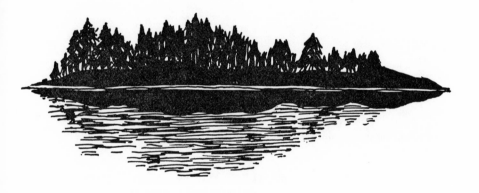

Paul Nelson

University Press of Virginia
Charlottesville

THE UNIVERSITY PRESS OF VIRGINIA
Copyright © 1982 by the Rector and Visitors
of the University of Virginia

First published 1982

Library of Congress Cataloging in Publication Data

Nelson, Paul, 1934–
  Days off.

  (Virginia Commonwealth University series for contem-
porary poetry)
  I. Title. II. Series.
PS3564.E474D3   1982   811'.54   82–20294
ISBN 0–8139–0965–1

Printed in the United States of America

Design by Janet Anderson

for Mom and Dad

FOREWORD

Even our enthusiasms—irrational surges of insight that overcome even the most joyless critic from time to time—sometimes require explanation, as in a case where a single book has been chosen above many fine contenders. In such a case the explanation, like the affinity itself, can only pretend to be objective. It will only be me telling you why I think this is a wonderful book.

I find Paul Nelson's poems remarkable on three scores, then. They are accessible, as accessible as the experience they spring naturally from. They are open-ended: the experience is enclosed in the structure of the poem, but at the end the door of that cage flies open, and the metaphor flies off in whatever direction your own analogy takes it. And third, the poems are gatherers (Robert Frost's word). They contain an unusual amount of life. An unusual percentage of the reality of the experience finds its way into them. We are used to (almost trained for, if we read the more cerebral critics, who will not tarry over *Days Off*, I predict) poems that *allude to* a marvelous variety of experience. Paul Nelson's poems *contain* a marvelous variety of experience.

I will try to demonstrate these three characteristics, but I can only do this in a way you may prefer to do for yourself, that is, by pointing to things in the poems. At this point, if I have run afoul of more than one of your prejudices, you may want to turn to the first poem and get on with the serious work of pleasure.

Nelson's accessibility seems to me a function of common sense, albeit the common sense of an uncommonly intelligent man. There is scarcely a poem in the collection that doesn't touch on a mystery, but always the mystery is presented literally for what it is, with as much matter-of-factness as in it lies.

In the poem called "Milking," for instance, the speaker is discovered at that task in a darkening barn, where many sense data confuse themselves vividly. The first stanza ends with the milker imagining the cow's death.

In the darkening barn, one bulb stares, flyspecked.
I squat the stool, press my brow against her loin.

She moans, already dripping in the pail.
I inhale the ammonia of hay and urine.
It doesn't clear my head. Instead, a foggy, white river
winds through a cheese-green valley,
grass still poking through the snow.
My hands mope between my knees, my eyes closed.
I rock my head against her meat.
She moans again, so my hands begin to work,
slow pistons shivering a hill. We heat.
I bleed this river into evening. My sweat
blends with slick where she has mopped herself.
Our teeth grind. Someday I will leave her hide
draped on the fence for birds to hammer the fat.

In the second stanza, we move from literal riddles to an irrational one that is to be apprehended where it arises, in the subconscious. We are ready for this: our attention has been alerted and directed and given confidence by having solved the sequence of sensations presented in the opening stanza.

The poem now seems to ask where the perimeters of the experience lie and, by extension, to ask how much we can know about the perimeters of any experience. This is a complex mystery to charge the last six lines of a short lyric with, and they are difficult lines for the reader to deal with, to hold in focus. But there is no mystification. The three sentences ask us to leap chasms, but the colloquial voice steadies us. The strategy used is apparent common sense: the speaker relates, with an idiom that conveys inevitability (as if we could deny it), two perfectly *sensible* impossible events, two fantasies about what he and the cow will do during the night. The thing told is as believable and accessible as a well told dream:

We stay awhile, lovers who have been considerate,
now spent and cooling. As if she wouldn't start
to eat all night, suck gallons of darkness up.
As if I wouldn't try to sleep and see,
the rods and cones beneath my lids
firing in their little baths of acid.

The opening-out of "Milking" is also characteristic of Nelson's work. Associations in this book tend to be not similes or even rangy metaphors so much as awarenesses of unseen connections. Look at the ending of "Wintering the Animals":

Look at the door. Imagine the animals,
blind and rocking in their stalls, pawing the double floor.
Can you hear the dry grind of their jaws? Go on,
unhook the stiff latch. If you can with your lax arms
shove it the other way. The animals steam by, out of the dead air
into the sunlight, then down across the meadow.

Beyond the broken fence they pause, looking back.
Stranger, you have emptied the barn again.
Not what you wanted.

How have we acquired that responsibility, idle readers who were merely standing by while the speaker ran on about his job of putting his animals in the barn before winter began? The closures of many of the poems are simultaneously disturbing openings.

What closes, in fact, is often a firm rhythmic cadence. See the last lines of "Getting Ready for the Trees," "Saith," "Holstein," or "The Parade"— a miracle of rhythm throughout. Many other poems end with longer sentences which provide the *sound* of closure in the act of reaching out, as we saw in "Milking."

Finally, by the containment of experience I mean only the powerful sensation of physical experience that accumulates in the book. We feel the several impacts of ice fishing, sauna, hawk dive, of wintering water snake and smothering in tent caterpillars. This containment is verbal, precise. In two poems ("Epithalamium" and "Confluences") he uses, and by usage defines, what I take to be a regional meaning of the word *riff*: a river shallow. This meaning is not given by most dictionaries, but it is by the poems where the word is used. And we are sent to the dictionary from time to time, as instructively as Berryman and Auden used to send us, and with as much pleasure, by other precisions. The words *engram, spicule, ziggurat, lumbar* are given back to us, temporarily anyhow, by pretty exactnesses, necessary to precise feeling.

If I'm not saying this well, who can describe containment like this?

I can tell a dog that has been rolling in shit
by the smile it wears
crossing the lawn toward me like a fundamentalist.

And let me raid the book once more, ending with "The Parade," a poem
that holds our Dionysian element and just possibly all of chaos.

Holt's old she-goat, with wide, yellow eyes,
her bag slapping her legs, paraded Potter's black
draft-horse, two ordinary cows, one chocolate bull,
assorted calves and kids, Jarule's golden retriever,
two pink swine and William, the town drunk,
to every house on Hardwood Ridge.
We peered from our windows and porches.
They plodded in the gardens, wandered in and out
of sheds and barns, pocked the lawns and septic fields.
We yelled, waved brooms, threw stones.
We called each other up. HAVE YOU SEEN THE ANIMALS?
or, THE ANIMALS ARE COMING! Now, they stand,
cropping the fields, or mute by fences,
snow riding their backs. The pigs wallow like William.
It was raining the day they came.
The children were in school.

WILLIAM MEREDITH

ACKNOWLEDGMENTS

The author and publisher wish to thank the following magazines, where certain poems first appeared:

Cincinnati Poetry Review, no. 8 (Spring 1981), for "Getting Ready for the Trees," reprinted by permission of the editor.

Crazyhorse, no. 19 (Fall 1979), for "Lives," reprinted by permission of the editor.

Denver Quarterly for "Traveling with Animals," "Bone Davening," and "Reasons for a Pond."

The Georgia Review for "Universal Donor."

The Goddard Journal for "The Day F.D.R. Died."

The Iowa Review 8/2 for "Wintering the Animals," reprinted by permission of the editor.

Ironwood for "Enduring the Thaw."

The Ohio Review for "The Mind Speaks of the Body."

Ploughshares for "The Lost World," "The Bat in His Room," "Cellars," "The Eleventh Man," "Milking," "The Snake in the Spring Box," and "Cleaning the Outhouse."

Seattle Review for "Holstein," "Broadtail Hawk," and "Seasonal."

The author wishes to thank the National Endowment for the Arts for its generous support.

CONTENTS

I

Lives	3
The Lost World	4
Traveling with Animals	5
Broadtail Hawk	6
Hip Boots, *for Cap't. Chas. O. Welch, 1888–1979*	7
Days Off	8
The Day F.D.R. Died	10
Saith	11
Getting Ready for the Trees	12
Making a Man	13
Cellars	15
The Eleventh Man	16
Returning to Water	17
Reasons for a Pond	18
Bone Davening	19
Sauna	20
The Mind Speaks of the Body	21
Taking Up a New Sport at Forty	22
Lobes	23
Milking	24
Wintering the Animals	25
Clearing	26
Jogger	27
Robins	29
Universal Donor	30

II

Enduring the Thaw	33
Frozen In	34
I–80	35

Ash   36
Confluences   37
April   38
For John Who Works with Retarded Children   39
Seasonal   40
Cassandra in Stone, Amyclae   41
The Daughter Pot   42
Fable, Maybe   43
Evening   44
Apologia   45
The Snake in the Spring Box   47

III

Holstein   51
The Parade   52
Imagining the Bone   53
The Bat in Your Room, *for Dave*   54
Epithalamium, *for Dave and Joni*   55
The Downed Horse   56
Night Out   57
Cleaning the Outhouse   58
The Tent Caterpillers   59
Focus   60
Sonnet   61
Endangered Species   62
Meditation   63
By a River in Southern Ohio   64
Following Fish   65
Shades Down and Porches Empty   66
The Tame Grieve   67
The Man Down the Road   68

I

LIVES

Wind baffles the lake this morning.
Halfway across, two figures in white hats
jiggle an aluminum skiff. One
squats near the outboard, fingering the moss
for a wax worm, which he hooks precisely,
then strips out line to stop the bait
six inches from the mud bottom.
This man catches fish, raps their heads on the gunwale
to stop the gasping. The other is me.

I used to fish.
Always has been me, hunched, looking idly at the windows
cradled by light that strikes the west shore.
Troubled by his lives, he will not see
one of them completed.

Outside their bed-size shacks, figures sit,
mummied in zippered suits, flicking wands
above the six-inch holes. In their palms
they will show you tiny gold and silver jigs from Sweden,
bits of neon sponge, a jar of pickled roe.
At their feet, buckets of live minnows
to be skewered and lowered in offering. In worse weather,
or night, they move inside to lamps and small stoves.
The lights shine out upon that waste as if they'd just
landed there, to take up homes. Today, the shore behind them
is a two-mile photograph in black and white, propped
on the dazzling stage. Such pleasure to see the fishermen
shift their stools, bend to skim the holes, do dances
against the cold. A week ago, a boy came plugging in,
across his arms a pike as long as his spine. He will never
get over the pain, draped and shivering, the long,
armed jaws still clapping the bait. But it is small fish
draws them out: croppies, like hand-painted Egyptian palettes;
yellow perch, elm leaves striped by sunlight . . .
jewelry in a lost time still glaring on the fisher mind,
snow beginning now, banishing the shore.

TRAVELING WITH ANIMALS

In May I drive east
to stand upon the sod, some faces I know
whose stone lids, lichened, look through me,
who keeps his innocence in transit.
I did worry, Tuesday, was it, that I passed you
like a note, your face so flimsy, headed west on 80.

We know each other's cars, how they sit the road.
I am a Volvo, intent upon the coming abstraction,
to wit, *to visit, to visit,* like tappets
ticking under the cap, that hate to stop
or start again.

I like it. I may love it: leather seats,
lumbar adjusted, radials soothing the road.
Semi's snore by, dynastically, on eighteen funereal wheels,
quiet enough beyond the tight window, air conditioning,
Coltrane on tape, whistling like a fish-bird in a rain forest.

Who wants the farm anymore? The porcelain packages of beef,
the wife-sucked baggies of broccoli? Not even the racked
fruit wines, cellared and cool, the spices
tied in little brooms in the pantry.

Racoons, fox stare from the roadside brush,
or pick at each other's mess, sealed near the line.
Up ahead, they idle from our way. Provincially,
crows flap above the wires.

BROADTAIL HAWK

Low in the field, on a spring of hardhack,
the hawk rides, big as a half-gallon of whiskey.
I idle at roadside, wondering if its meal
lies under, cooling in the stubble.

The calmness of the beast, having killed, calms me.
Its head swivels slowly, appraising.
It lifts one wing, folds it neatly,
dressing for dinner. I stay in my cover, nearly asleep.
The yellow eyes have spotted my nature: harmless
putterer in grain . . . liar:

I have killed: pig, deer, chickens, ducks,
goat, mice, geese, rats, steer, snakes, fish, frogs,
crabs, trees, and once, a hawk. I blew it from the air.
My dog finished it, her head buried in the arbor of wings.
I went to school with one of its yellow legs,
cinched upon a blue aggie, tied to my belt.

I'd make a run for it, but the idea of air
concussive above me has jellied my knees.
The gracious curve of talons
completes itself in meat. I nap now,
hooked on this pleasure.

HIP BOOTS

for Capt. Chas. O. Welch, 1888–1979

Hanging from their nails
as if a man were descending through the shed roof.

What's light and vacant rises. The real thing,
down to one pound for every year he's lived,
hardly distresses the sheets. A young nurse
lifts him easily, who was a bucking weight, to his chair
to keep his lungs from filling up
with a couple tablespoons of mud.
What he wants to do is lie there,
with what's left of sweat and meat
press up against the ceiling, down into his wife,
friends all gone before,
decades of dogs and weedy gardens.

Doctor comes down, clean-shaven, smocked in white,
says, "Charles, how are we today?" On her knees,
nurse cranks up the bed. His mouth is a hole,
open to the air, the stars, like flies.
He stares, scared by his boots,
twisting slowly in the door behind the doctor's head.

We could cut them down, fold them in the corner,
or hang them by their ankles. But boots are saved
by being upright, free to flue the essence,
as if a man were risen,
pop-eyed in the dark above the rafters.

DAYS OFF

Swimming the brackish rip,
I flood with infant dropsy into summer.
Light glances off the pilings underneath
funneling the shapes of friends, green citizens,
who dive and twist akimbo. Refreshed,
we all sail out to see the seals bask.
Live stones, body bags, they cough and bark like elders,
hauling themselves in and out of the surf,
a million years deciding. The pups, marble-white,
slide out beneath the shadow of the sail,
tail-walk, like cane heads, to see us skim, as if
we were their souls.

Last week, pacing the bridge rail, way above the mast,
a man yelled down, blazing in the noon aura,
nor could I hear well for the squalling gulls,
my outboard gargling. I circled in the channel,
getting dizzy, finally saw his fishline slice,
laserlike . . . cut the engine, drifted over,
pulled the humming monofilament. Slow,
that life below, steering in the dark, rose.
The black socketed head broke water, yawning.
I let it go.

As I have always let go.
Then pulled again. Again the head,
the whiskered lip skewered by the hook,
a bit of herring on the steel leader.
The animal half pulled itself over the gunwale.

I snipped the shank. It dropped back,
resurfaced, looked at me
awed by light.

Shaved and similar without their teeth,
the dying, too, get cute. Oiled by nurse for passage,
they lighten with the wish to rise. Anna,
who lost her husband years ago,
forgets features of her loved one's face.
In her crib, she gawks at another in heaven.

Had the man on the bridge jumped,
had I fished him out, dead or alive,
his eyes would be fixed with reflection.
And I would still be standing in a boat.
Reeling in, he yelled again.
I waved him off, slipped downstream,
yanking the starter.

THE DAY F.D.R. DIED

Mr. Paradise circles the back bank of Nine
on the eight-foot mower, then sweeps the pond's edge,
strafing. I am knee-deep, like a peasant in a rice paddy,
groping for balls with my toes. Then my mother is calling,
blond tones from the dead-end street where the fairway
joins it like peace and quiet.
We half-sleeve the small flag with Dad's black sock,
fix it to the porch. That night the men stand talking
underneath the light where the backboard is spiked to the pole.
We lie flat in the sandtrap. Schmidt has a tracer from France.
Richie has three wooden matches and Barbara, lying next to me,
smells new. Mr. Dokas backs out for the night shift.
His lights scan the sand and green. We leap up yelling,
charge past our fathers and vanish under the trees
of various lawns.

SAITH

My father and I walked out of the sun
under the high firs on beds of decomposing needles
through which "le coq" mushrooms fired with a bit of color.
I did not think that they were poisonous.
I never thought that he was thinking,
just passing in and out of light with me.
I simply guessed him spent when I was ten.

We emerged on the dusk-lit road, the gray Ford
a silver capsule, a heap of rust by now
or smelted into other forms.
On the way home the steering chattered.
We interpreted together, he appreciating
my rendition of the lore: "The front end is shot."
Saith.

So the problem is that sex is difficult as art.
We bare our asses and our troubles in our beds
with a little bit of color.
The front end *was* shot.

GETTING READY FOR THE TREES

We walk out into the evening's pale field
that we burned five years ago. Friendly now,
we are too old to be of so much interest to each other.
I complain about the hardhack, moss and alders,
how I must have animals and time to love this land.
You say it just grows up, your breath
hard and fatherly beside me.

We find a little tamarack, the tree
that loses its hair in a shower of gold.
And twin birches, tall as the fence, as young brothers.
You want them for your lawn, to watch them.
The light thins. The trees call back their shadows,
but we stay with evening anyway. Your shoulders
bunch. It has gone cool,
time to burn again.

Spading a dim circle around their roots, I cut the ends
to make them double-sprout, stronger for transplanting.
In the cuts I sift a little dung.
We will return a month from now to take them,
when the rains come.

There is nothing to protest. Your tight, heroic image
wanders into hay a distance off. Once, before I shot,
I whistled at a deer, grazing over there.
The year's last grass. Now, I squint to see you, dimly,
recalling me. It did not lift its head.

MAKING A MAN

I stared into the husk of the Nike Temple.
The wingless lady, lugged off by Englishmen,
was carved that way to keep the spirit in town.
Moonlight glinted from my new braid.

I drank red wine. By midnight, shadow hags
shagged light across the grounds,
one of whom appeared to me, offering her mystery.
Draped in black, her teeth two plates of ochre wood,
she wanted my Timex.

What would it have meant to take a crone
on Athena's pedestal? Would mind
stand still for that, forty feet tall,
a painted lady with jewels for eyes? Wise and just?
I shooed her into oblivion.

At the same time thought I saw a caryatid
take a few virtuous steps in Attic dance.
I was that young, wanting women on the porch, or Ithaca,
that moonlight in me. I loved my ships,
gray sarcophagi with lights, riding Ephtherios Bay.

Maidens and goddesses wear away. Other men
have taken them in, out of the rain.
Acid has eaten their eyes, abstracted their curls and folds.
The polychrome madonnas go wan and blind above their babies.
In China, the porcelain princess needs a paint job.
Kali, in shadow, has termites.

I sailed away next morning without love or battle.
We left in formation, flags up, popping in wind,
whistles blowing for the president of Greece,
a trim little killer in a Paris suit, the acropolis in sun
a pile of cinnamon bones.
I could not climb into that bright night,
and girls from Piraeus waved from the pier,
awed by the departure of swine.

CELLARS

A black iron stove with white, china handles,
my grandmother, croned at fifty and exiled to the cellar
by death and daughter, talking to herself in tongues
above a blue flame, her legs wrapped, her shoes
clumsy as jars. She can't pick up the nails and screws,
or screw the Gerber bottles back into their caps,
nailed overhead by her husband, like gasps to the kitchen floor.
Her hands hook into themselves.

An uncle, living by himself in a trailer court,
was once on an Egyptian dig, has breathed air
trapped for 3000 years. I have been to Mycenae,
under the helmet of Agamemnon's tomb, built underground
by reasonable children. I tried to walk a tunnel there
to reach the secret spring, source against the sieges.
Eight feet in, I ran against a shield of blue flies,
humming like arrows and mourners.

In my own hole, an emerald hose coils at the foot of the stairs.
Two white tanks loom along the wall
and the soapstone sink hangs like an open jaw.
At the far end, a door as high as a dwarf
leads into the bin where specks of coal still flicker
in the light that smears the tiny window, outside of which
the brilliance of a Buick hubcap buckles my knees.

THE ELEVENTH MAN

In the headlights, a wet, wild boy,
leaping and yelling like a state champ,
pointing his finger at the river.
I jockeyed the yellow beams across the spray of guardwire.
By then I was not there, but saw the roof of the car,
like snow riding a boulder, heard country-western
drifting in, the radio still playing fifty feet from shore.
And the kid, crazed to the waist, calling me into
the summer syrup.

I move too slowly, surely now, half-submerged in mind.
Recently, another woman died.
I carried her, lobbing her red life on my shirt.
I happened to be there, too:
4-wheel drive in warm rain, a universal donor on a mud road.

But now I sat in the sand, removing my shoes,
shed my pants as well, then waded in, cheered on,
the tepid water mouthing my balls.
Why not, for loveliness, wade a river at night?

Look, a basketball rolls on a varnished floor
in its own highlights. Though ten tall men
dive for it, each is the eleventh, beside himself.
The boy cried out, "She isn't in the car!"
I said "where" to the river, was listening to the music
when it swallowed once and drowned.

RETURNING TO WATER

Tonight, the river swims with lemming lights,
flashing and vanishing, bright sorties.
I want survivors, heroes to surface, not
people from the village, a neighborhood dog,
a kid who slipped at the falls.

Once, I pulled my knees up into my arms,
settled, releasing my air into the sleeves and scarves
that reached so idly upward, sewn to some exhausted log.
Submarined in green light, I opened my mouth to speak
(I still have something to say) then pulled away,
kicking at local specters.

I surfaced just beneath the float, coughing fists,
sounding the hardwood boards,
safe among the fifty-gallon drums.

REASONS FOR A POND

Across the road, warted with rocks,
poplars lift to no particular sky.
Top leaves whip and flitter in a Russian wind,
slaughtering itself, dropping on the fireweed and hardhack,
on cellar stones so old that no one
claims them for their people.

June rains and the big racoon brings along a daughter,
nesting in the other rotten eave, to fight with at night,
in the attic ruins of furniture and rugs,
waking the dogs until I stop them with a light.
I shot them, finally, from the roof.
It was the smell of piss, fish and clamflat in the house.
I pried the fascial boards to reach the blind
amphibious pups, squealing and sucking my knuckles.
You held the black plastic bag.

Animals and stones. I can't leave them be
because they won't leave me,
but outlive the house, our dogs, the silences we make.
In the center of the field, I am bulldozing a pond,
irregular in shape, consuming trees, the cellar hole,
to draw from secretive springs
water to reflect that sky.

BONE DAVENING

Something of a dog with dead things, I sniff
the road-smashed toad, cherishing the brilliant
garbage of release, of blue, gutted snake.
I don't exactly roll in it, but have that sachet
to greet you.

I find the icons of surprise, of power and disgrace,
pyred on the leaves: antlers in a nest of apples,
a fox skull glowing in a boulder's shade, the startled jaws
symmetrically unhinged . . . or by the fence
a shot-pocked washtub with a bleached head inside,
green grass streaming from the nostrils. And once,
incisors, burnt orange, like an Indian baby's bracelet
on a bed of quills. Bird wings, paired as if embrace
had laid them down.

Flesh swings and drapes the spoons and clubs,
takes on the print of corduroy and buttons.
Coral blooms, a hardship in the knees and fingers.
The tympanum creaks, thickens under pressure,
but we want to dive the Barrier Reef, crystal and easy
as the shadow drifting underneath, our minds
insoluble marrow, free as the pale, reflecting fish.

SAUNA

Outside the little cedar, two-bit hell,
the locker room is cool, blue tile.
Doors occasionally clang. The mirrors do not fog
but run clear above the pile of white, decomposing towels.

I have taken my body here.
We sit in the basement of a fine old hotel
waiting for the heat to rise inside,
that we might enter the sanctum.
The red light winks we may be purified.

Sighing on the bench, we drift into another body,
of wood and soil, the community stench.
Alone together, we whisper "Hero." Fighter pilot
in the cockpit under fire. Commander,
fifty fathoms down and sinking, torpedoed and penitent.
My own water boils my eyes.
My god, why have I forsaken me?

We call it a day. Beer, sex, the job all down the drain.
It is difficult to lift a hand,
a foot to pull a sock. Upstairs,
cooling in the lobby, we did not expect to live this much,
one towel to a person.

THE MIND SPEAKS OF THE BODY

I caught it again this morning,
having slipped the coast of sleep,
making way through locks to another ocean,
driving waves against the nations
and shuddering the parked cars. Far inland,
nurseries jiggle with suspicion.
Babies love it. Women see
the world's longest bedsheet, a hull
frozen on the line, while men fear the thick shafts
driving in their guts, the huge screws
screwing just below the surface.
Even when I had it docked there were complaints:
it blocked the view of Jersey,
refused to roll over like the *Normandie*.
I have loved this luxury, but it sails without me
sometimes, takes women to Bermuda, returns to port
to have its bottom scraped, bilges pumped,
a new skin of white paint. Then it swings
on the great Navy anchor, taking on fuel,
getting lower and lower in the water,
the finest ship afloat.

TAKING UP A NEW SPORT AT FORTY

I haven't the cool, miss easy ones, my arms boiling the air.
I don't move smoothly in the center of the court,
do not court the passing shot, but lunge at low ones
like a kid in the back seat with the town pump.
But I'm born again, on a strange floor, varnished
with spohrosyne and sweat, where women playing racketball
have left their odor, where I get lean, sharper,
more and more slowly, as the ball twists with English,
no longer my language. I am that man flailing,
gasping as the ball is a gasp on the back wall,
or springs beyond my reach. I am that man pacing the hall,
carrying his gloves and a tin of balls, looking for a match.
I am not looking for a partner. This isn't marriage.
I am looking for a hooker. We will play through centuries,
keeping the covenant of pain. We will never learn
to care for one another, but for a "kill," deep in the corner.
Wise men will visit us, stand in the balcony,
ignorant of how we fall toward epiphany,
a black hole hustling in the universe.

LOBES

He says he hears from the left side only.
You change chairs. But in the middle of your story
his eyes glaze. He does not read your lips,
is drawn to music in another room.

I, too, am defective, my ears flat against my head,
the dog that has crapped in the chapel.
If I look right at you, seem eager, your words
fly by like owls. However, if I cock my head,
avert my eyes, I am listening.

I envy his deprivation,
what the bright side desires: sunny discourse and wit,
critical acumen and manly curses.
He travels in moonlight to the left, music in his whole
cranium, sweet as the odor of women.

Joking, he gives me his right side, the crumpled ear.
I stare like a gunfighter.
He hums. I jabber.
We both know that southpaw who sits in dusk,
who was light, whose loss of heaven gave us art.

MILKING

In the darkening barn, one bulb stares, flyspecked.
I squat the stool, press my brow against her loin.
She moans, already dripping in the pail.
I inhale the ammonia of hay and urine.
It doesn't clear my head. Instead, a foggy, white river
winds through a cheese-green valley,
grass still poking through the snow.
My hands mope between my knees, my eyes closed.
I rock my head against her meat.
She moans again, so my hands begin to work,
slow pistons shivering a hill. We heat.
I bleed this river into evening. My sweat
blends with slick where she has mopped herself.
Our teeth grind. Someday I will leave her hide
draped on the fence for birds to hammer the fat.

We stay awhile, lovers who have been considerate,
now spent and cooling. As if she wouldn't start
to eat all night, suck gallons of the darkness up.
As if I wouldn't try to sleep *and* see,
the rods and cones beneath my lids
firing in their little baths of acid.

WINTERING THE ANIMALS

Shove the big door on its greased track
shutting in the dark for winter. It isn't easy.
The barn sags, south eaves braced for ice.

April, the place seems smaller, leaning from the sun
toward the meadow. The north posts sink through frost;
bald trees bare the hill.
We are the first ones down this season
and we know the earth is dying.

Look at the door. Imagine the animals,
blind and rocking in their stalls, pawing the double floor.
Can you hear the dry grind of their jaws? Go on,
unhook the stiff latch. If you can with your lax arms
shove it the other way. The animals steam by, out of the dead air
into the sunlight, then down across the meadow.

Beyond the broken fence they pause, looking back.
Stranger, you have emptied the barn again.
Not what you wanted.

CLEARING

Leaving the yeasty, drowsing heat of the kitchen,
I walk back behind the shed, into the last evening light.
Gulls flap along the sunburned horizon,
melding with bruised bay water, above my toy meadow.

I cleared this field of third, maybe fourth full growth
twenty years ago, when I wondered at folk
who let it go to such profusion. I still owe awe
to the threat it makes to keep on waking up a wilderness,
answer hay and spirea, berry-canes and alder with scythe,
animals and lime, as if I were grace, or rain,
as if the gulls, returning in the morning from rookeries at sea,
do so because I wish them well.

I stretch in bed at night, aching with sanity, sore with health,
listening to the roots, the suckers in the sod,
all those fingers yearning, beyond
my clear accomplishment.

JOGGER

Around the lake
makes a three-mile track.
I go sewing this ellipse,
stitching in the houses
like buttons on the bank,

hemming a lack
by looking in the windows: lamps
and golden bedposts, a child in blue
pillowed in a chair, the cars outside

squatting on their cushions,
quiet life that I squeeze by,
good felony abroad on starstruck
winter nights.

Taking their lives, I am just
the sneakers vanishing
beyond the garbage and the mail,
in, then out of a neighbor's light.

Dogs come out from sleep,
appear along my side and then drop off,
satisfied. None bark.

Today, between the cottages, I see the fishermen.
They violate the ice, make dark, irregular trails.
I try to contain them but they leak.
They kneel and fish, play with string, enameled
jigs and feathered eyes.

I consider the figure eight.
I could obliterate them, X the whole lake,
signal-in a storm to drive them home,
to make things plain again.

Oh, I hear them calling to each other,
singing from their snow stools, way out
in the middle of waste. I run circles around them,
have yet to settle for baubles and weights,
to chisel and sit, chisel and sit,
peering into a hole.

ROBINS

Two robins stand on the garden hose
looking west. One's head, cocked,
imagines a rumble in the track.
Now a third, all heads up,
triple hop to shade.

To be this busy on a summer morning,
to wish for nothing but what arrives,
stretch, peer between the blades of iris,
stare with calculable diffidence
at a passing caterpiller, its confreres
all over the garage like punctuation.
To not be culpable, unfaithful or old.

When their sky-colored shells
flake, yolk-stuck to the walk,
or nests are jay-ravaged,
scattered in the vetch,
they start all over again, though first frost
stiffens the early worm. The fledglings,
quite speckled children of a second mating,
try to age in time
to catch the irrevocable flight.

They start all over again.
They wish for nothing.
They are back again along the hose.
I sneak out and turn it on.
They step back, listen to the worm,
look at one another, then fly up,
knowing the difference
between one thing and another.

UNIVERSAL DONOR

I license the State to take from roadside
any of my parts, flesh or vegetable, to keep cool
and give them back in time. But,

if a woman with my heart meets a man with my kidney,
the child born is mine. Who takes my lungs must run.
They sag on minor inspiration.

To have my heart and eyes is worst, to love
as if one never had. She will look back,
love that other harder.

If a man with my spleen meets a man with my eyes,
it will be knives. One with both might suicide
on half my fascination with release. I *was* driving.

If you are, in part, my remains, invent me,
like one of the old gods. Be for my lady's sake
my shaman. Speak with tongues, some obeisance

to one so severed from a life that has also stricken you.
Refuse my liver, old liquor-sieve. I do not grant my brain.
It aches too much remembering my disposition.

II

ENDURING THE THAW

Cars swim a little in the softening road.
Spicules of piss, like glass tusks, crush in the pig yard.
The maples have started to leak. Up two ramps,
in the second loft, the air is semitropical by noon.
The sheep have been there since New Years, buried in the mow,
dropping lambs.

Combing the hay, I fish one out. It kicks against my chest,
then calms as the ewe stares. I have begun to resent my feet,
such citizens, yearning for the dark of shoes.

Who exactly loves the animals?
Baits the sow beneath the falls and gun
with slices of Wonderbread? Who strains
to heave the shaved thing skyward on the whiffletree?
And whose porch here
hangs with infant carcasses, stiffening overnight?

When I think of women who can do these things
I want to take one in my arms . . . caped and lean,
glossy and hard as leaf lard
before the rendering.

FROZEN IN

The lake has gone to glass.
In wind, one wave froze, making a fault
reaching to the northern shore
where the estates stand back and boats
are humble on the lawns.
The cottage is still. I could work
but for the smell of oak leaves
like women burning in the neighborhood,
cloudy and romantic. It is too cold
to open all the windows, too warm in here
to make the bed, all riven by my nightly travel.
The car is bored in the drive. I'm out of milk
and the coffee has an acid streak.

If I close one eye and block the fissure with the lamp,
the lake is healed, my miracle. But there's
a woman walking over there, in dungarees and a red jacket.
The sun strikes her hair; she has studied dance.
A dog leaps awkwardly beside her,
and just now she pauses at the other end
of the sealed message I have sent my wife.

A dull, strict run in Illinois, framed by
religious fields, wide as New England towns,
and then the Mississippi, where it buckles the land,
brings it to its knees for water, where the long span
near Bettendorf chutes me toward Des Moines like a steer,
toward sunset pink with fertilizer
hogging down on the black continent.
The old car strains at 4000 r.p.m. I want this over with;
against that sky, small fluorescent rips in the canvas,
jet trails with their own perspective over Omaha.
The coffee is gone; I don't dare open the bottle,
but hallucinate anyway: my wife raped, my dog shot
in the maudlin storefront we are renting. My wife gone,
I am free, shake that off, and yet resent the tolls,
the sophrosyne, where there are no wrong moves
when a semi towers by, shuddering like a girl, the long,
flatbed body flexing beneath its central load, a crate
chained and painted gray as the Ark of the Covenant
while huge green combines crawl the everlasting corn
in tendance, and I am sucked along in the truck's wake,
saving gas but doing eighty, considering the exits:
Tipton, Solon, West Liberty, the disposition of lamps
in the farmhouse windows, a figure with a platter in her hands,
how once, on a back road, I saw a blue man sitting naked,
a blue piano propped open beside him, and then her hair,
blue on the blue satin pillow, watching the same blue vision . . .
and I wake again, still wedded to the road,
passing through the shadow of a grain elevator,
two miles from this home.

ASH

We put aside a daughter: shoebox of ashes
tucked beneath a fruit tree
that half-bloomed in sandy soil behind the barn.

Locals said her life was with another man.
"In His home," they said, "she is His tree."
He climbs her, this sufferer,
his heart that wan.

Jesus on the tree! The unfinished son,
an idea's hand. He should have been an April girl,
the father squat as Job, her heart on the right side,
as if she backed into the world, facing up to the past.

We sold that house and land.
No family man, I cut, we burned the struggling tree.
Ashes, they say, to ashes.
Something went out of us then, but love,
I cover another man's daughter.

CONFLUENCES

Summer people stop, look on
while the White and the Mad run scores of miles
through a Vermont valley named by Indians,
then join here in rafts of whey, sliding by
Boardman's Texaco, the grammar school,
its old pipe drooling. The marriage
has no offshoots. No streams enter.
Where they have come together, they have come together,
a silent widening, and those who stop to look
do not look at one another but continue down
past the acre yard of sawdust where the icehouse
loomed throughout our youth, where I still moon,
believing in ice.

Quiet, the reeds that hem the shore.
Black ducks steer in pairs. Herons stalk the riffs.
I kneel and shove my fingers into what is left,
the sawdust earth, still cool, to feel that colder marriage.
We are there, stiff as usual, just beginning to speak.
It has taken our lives. We are amazed,
children in the glacial barn; the stars that melt all day
harden bright all night.

Each in a blue, shivering channel,
we peered into the half-wiped cakes that kissed and froze,
confusing themselves with each other, with
their own breaths. That was play.
You give me your hand, still warm as summer water,
as love, that never settles anything.

She says "lilacs seep." Points at last year's slime,
calls it "algaebloom," at small pink lichens
eating mortar in the walls. Last night,
driving, small animals were "candies,"
sealed near the yellow line. She sucks air, thrilled,
as a great blue heron slices into the marsh,
squawks, looks for something to spear.
I do not want to make another child.

In the shed, on the scalded spot,
I have stood above the animals, bleeding them.
They draw in around a blade
the way the earth tries to absorb the human,
then relaxes. I have relaxed. Ten years ago,
I stirred the ashes of our child with my finger,
studying that terrain as if it were the moon's.

She gets this way in April, while I still
cut myself quite absently, amazed at dishes
blushing in the sink. I can't remember the child's name.
Winter? Spring? Beyond the kitchen window,
my own face rises fatuously, in the back yard,
glowing in the lilacs.

FOR JOHN WHO WORKS WITH
RETARDED CHILDREN

The alternative is to have none,
to exorcise, the mother kneeling by the little tub
beginning to rinse, pushing it down,
no pity for the heat-vague eyes.
Or the young husband, pacing waxed floors in the sun-room
where the incubator glows like a brain in hemorrhage.
He could end the marriage now, stagger into the snowy
parking lot and drive away. Four, five days at least
without grief, drunk as a cow in clover.
Once, I stood in the window of my cottage,
ten feet from the porch next door,
watching a big, red-faced kid
kick his mongoloid sister in the back
until his glasses fell off. For seconds
I said *yes*. Yes, but rushed out and called him
animal names, threatened to beat him to death
until the intelligence returned to his eyes.

SEASONAL

Summer nights I ran like a lie, long strides,
then stopped, my mouth wide open to the moon,
my ears awake to the clicking of bats.
Off again, down the fairway to the woods,
dodging trees to the brief dam that ends the pond,
then into the cool hall of the icehouse.

I stood there until my breath
grew small as the tiny ziggurat of ice
hiding in the northwest corner, then climbed the beams
to lie flattened in the moldered hay on the second loft
where my life could love itself completely,
as the moon bloomed lemon through the broken roof.

Today, on the icehouse dock in front of the cottage,
my neighbor's mongoloid daughter, paralyzed in fat
and blue snowsuit, who, of all people should know better,
points and waves across the decomposing surface,
directing ducks in low, lunar vowels,
the birds circling in from the maudlin south.

CASSANDRA IN STONE, AMYCLAE

Knowledge doesn't come the way it used to, like bad food
I'd simply emit, or blood that I could smell,
quickening in the dining hall.
I have begun to predict for myself, in my mouth
a mineral sound that isn't kinetic in the sanctuary hedges,
moonlit. Rising again, the one pocked breast is dumb,
however miraculous. Certainly not in the stifled gas
inside a wooden horse.

I don't remember *why* the curse. Gods and men, likely.
Yes, it is bad, very expensive to have to say what you know,
which you always know before somebody else. Better
to court silence. Poets have figured that,
like middle-aged men who travel, then want to come home.

I was on Clyt's side. My lovely head, the bleating twins,
drained like vain words into the crust of Mycenae.
Well, we all know how to be deaf by now, and I'm too old
to go around screaming anymore.

Except, this stone tongue wrestles behind the shut gates.
Beyond grief, I may speak. Not today.

THE DAUGHTER POT

Shaped on a dirt floor
the child rounds, wet, glistening
like a belly.
Another improbable birth? Yes.

The crone watches it squint in the April sun,
witnesses it squat there, enduring its glaze,
taking on hues. Its mouth is wide open to flies,
to rain, to voices still drifting that region
like the ashes of Thera.

The crone sees into the past: large, clay-sealed hulls,
the hot flash of armor, her groin, rendered.
Her hands feel a little less rigid this morning,
her knees maybe possible. She looks at the pot,
the little daughter, says "Whore," and gives in,
out of the large, red-faced wind,
to the idiocy of goats.

Eras later, the daughter lies on her side.
The sea slips by again and again, like her own
clear content. Coarse but lovely, with one
painted, amber eye, she listens to villages fail,
catching the smell with the laughter.

FABLE, MAYBE

A rabbit worked under the chicken wire,
stunted the lettuce. She said "Shoot it!"
All the rabbits. Mornings, on the back porch,
in the first chartreuse light, I watched.
I imagined things, my own innocence,
fondling the gun.

This morning, a tallish creature hopped in the rows.
Dawn glowed pink through its leaf-veined ears.
The gun felt like a pole, which I pointed at the garden.
The quiet shifted in the hay. Swallows chittered on the line.
My own failures in the world were pleasant.
She said "Shoot!" The explosion tipped the earth.
The air was full of crazed birds. One leg kicking,
the raked carcass screwed in the dirt.
Lettuce draped the fence.

She walked into the house, disgusted.
Compelled as usual, I walked toward it.
The dog sniffed indifferently the tick-infested thing,
legs shattered and akimbo, bleeding from the nose and ears.
Its eyes were popped like the philosopher at Z.
In my palm, it weighed as much as a baby,
which I tossed into the ditch for fox, ravens, racoons.
I walked back into the kitchen, hung up my gun, said
"We started the world this morning."
She said, "I will not live to see it die."

EVENING

He hunkered on the grass, his golden haunches
shivering. I stared back, combed my hair.
He had just named a day full of animals
and had that look of triumph and captivity.
I offered him a drink. He sipped, said the house
was filthy, the garden full of weeds. *Weeds*
he's named them, his brow clutched in nameless
urgency, like some constipated angel.
I wanted to talk, but his eyes flew over the wall,
over the tree. Always the Open. So, that night,
after he ate, I taught him the fruits of my body.
He thrived.

APOLOGIA

She wasn't my idea.
I was too green to be lonely, too
wide-eyed to see my own bone bloom.
I ate in front of the refrigerator,
satisfied with my nakedness,
the little light inside.

I could already name things,
as if my breathing made them run.
I squawked *stork*; it said *stork*.
A gesture on my part.

I said "Eve?"
She smiled first.
What I felt I still can't name.
The loss was that great.

After the eviction, she took lovers.
She found a job: Sumer, Babylon,
Delphi. It was O.K. She called;
we talked on the phone for hours,
me in front of the open door
as if it were a casket
picking at yesterday's lasagna.

Cain was her favorite.
Abel was a little dull like me.
I couldn't forgive, not knowing
what "dead" was, until then a predilection

I couldn't imagine. She seemed to understand,
buried one and loved the other.
Said she *wanted* her life. I didn't know how
to *want* my life.

She says I am a new man.
I wonder what would happen if I lifted
the other rib. You know, just put it out in the sun?

THE SNAKE IN THE SPRING BOX

Cold-blooded, the surface just above its head
is collared light, ragging my reflection
in a blinding lace of ice, below which it lifts
like an insulated wire. I roll my sleeve,
reach down and pinch its neck, hard as a bullet,
then draw upward, dragging the tail from under a brick.
Slowly, I coil its weight against my stomach,
beneath my numb palm.

I wait. But my body doesn't warm it.
In my hands there is no urgency or struggle,
just the forked, involuntary language,
stabbing at what's white.
It isn't cold but sleeping.

I started out to shovel snow,
lift the lid to see the water, the mud
like pollen on the bottom
after too many blank months. The light
had somehow unwound it. Or had it started on its own
to beat the season? I drop it back.
The spring slashes, then calms.
Down there, coiling beyond my reflection,
it won't recall a thing of me,
as when a child is borne
from bed to bed in a stranger's arms.

III

HOLSTEIN

Her back is a hillock of snow, thoughtless
and decomposing in the clover, over stones.
Whistle and she will rise, come swaying
to force her chartreuse tongue into your pocket
to root for little apples. She will bat her fly-stuck eyes
and rasp the sweat from your arms.
You will sleep better for that kiss.

THE PARADE

Holt's old she-goat, with wide, yellow eyes,
her bag slapping her legs, paraded Potter's black
draft horse, two ordinary cows, one chocolate bull,
assorted calves and kids, Tarule's golden retriever,
two pink swine and William, the town drunk,
to every house on Hardwood Ridge.
We peered from our windows and porches.
They plodded in the gardens, wandered in and out
of sheds and barns, pocked the lawns and septic fields.
We yelled, waved brooms, threw stones.
We called each other up. HAVE YOU SEEN THE ANIMALS?
or, THE ANIMALS ARE COMING! Now, they stand,
cropping the fields, or mute by fences,
snow riding their backs. The pigs wallow like William.
It was raining the day they came.
The children were in school.

IMAGING THE BONE

I expect you to be home. Though no one is that innocent.
Not the mutt on the porch that trekked three states,
grave ravines and two thick rivers with your newspaper.
A smart dog begs with its head,

eyes the cupboard door, imagining the bone,
but won't roll over or play dead . . . gets stiff instead,
gray in the muzzle, takes blind love in covenant,
but can't take friendship, the mere consistency, the price

always up. Like period furniture, one lives with it,
because expecting much is far too calculated. I confess.
I'd enter your house again, sniff, piss to mark my place,
take a big antique piece and leave. The whole cupboard!

Worn by hands, oiled by your skin, even Hubbard's
bares what we can never have, offered too easily perhaps
to gratify any of us, who don't scratch, won't whine
to be fetched in or out, because a friend is just

a surprise . . . a blue-tick hound, so gaunt with running bear
I guessed it came to me to die. Fed meat and meal,
blessing me with one moon eye, it curled behind the stove.
By dawn it broke the screen. I heard it in the hills, sing.

THE BAT IN YOUR ROOM

for Dave

You were five. It inhabited your clothes in the closet
or flopped by the shell lamp that jittered on the ceiling.
You screamed when I caught it in my trout net
where it clicked and gagged and laced itself into the trammel,
its mouth a lipstick heart on a gorilla's face.
You hit me with your fists; I laughed and cut the strings,
opened the window and set it on the sill,
loose in the dismembered mesh.
The night air fell in, stilled it, a small purse
drawn about its coins. Some creatures can't be saved
and live.

EPITHALAMIUM

for Dave and Joni

Drenched leaves, Indian heat
canopy the brook, a turning
green tunnel that you crouch along
from rock to rock, feeding the yellow line,
the transparent leader, the preposterous fly
onto the riffs and pools. Chicken feathers,
cotton fixed to steel, a dash of red for decoration, maybe blood.

It is difficult to keep the thing afloat,
to keep the line from foolishness with alders,
to keep your temper as filaments of web
grace your eyes, your nose, your lips.
In the open, when you simply cast about
it always seemed so easy, all you had to do

was lie there, finning in the current,
and everything you needed came along
to your lovely gullet. All you had to do
was open wide, or look up
to see what's on the surface, what can be taken
with an easy rise . . . while you kept cool,
grew more beautiful: bright orange fins,
red jewels, a streak of silver by the gash of gill.

Here it is, larger than life, just floating along,
twitching a little, your nervous meal, coming to hand,
trying not to belly up. But, you do not know
who is hooked, your hand or the fish
as that weight slides into your palm,
and yet, everyone is fed.

THE DOWNED HORSE

In the field, a crowd rings a big white boulder,
talking to it with their hands. Some kneel.
Coming close, we hear the warden swear,
Sam whisper in the flattened ear.
A rifle lies in the grass and the children pale.

We have not known this beast, standing for years in the open.
It grazed in weeds where wire hid, strapping its pasterns,
and though we've clipped the wire, salved the sopped legs,
it will not reconsider. We anger now, at this will
to stare beyond the mountains, stone-eyed westward,
over the whole cooling ball.

Then a child in the barn bangs a grain pan.
The horse bolts, stands shuddering among us.
Now we could shoot, cheapened to have thought
the race would go on thrashing.

NIGHT OUT

Blank by the fire.
Coals dropped in platelets. My hands glowed,
years fused. So I got up and drove out the forest road
as if I were a star beneath the jittery stars,
swarming the mountainous sofas.

Thirty below, 2 A.M., I missed the turn beyond the bridge,
slid once around, hallucinated into a drift.
The hood popped. The engine-well filled with snow.
I hadn't been drinking but sat there
thinking how the beauty of that night would freeze in my eyes.
It was then the moose came from the trees, wading,
waving its great, palmated rack, looming above the car.
It looked in, lowered its neck, hooked the rocker panel
and with something of a moan flipped me over, out of the snow,
into the middle of the road, snorted and walked off upside down.
I sat on my neck. I couldn't see the sky,
was wondering, sorry when the headlights came,
the Atlantic Seafood truck for Portland, turning me yellow,
a yolk in a cracked egg, almost running me over.
He jimmied the door. I spilled out talking.
He wouldn't believe me any more than you,
how I'd been saved, that my life had been in danger.
The tracks were gone in powder. All-State
looked at the buckled roof but would not call it
an act of God or Man, wouldn't swallow Moose.
But that big, sad face, rubber-lipped above me,
moons in my dreams.

CLEANING THE OUTHOUSE

By August the remains will be a rope in dust,
a theology, a brown snake too limp with sun to struggle.
I return it to the house, unless its rotten, and
consider the year, the hole that gapes in the seatboard.
How emptied I must be, day after day.

Easter on, I feed the rope into the new heap,
coiling it in with a stick, mashing the pyramid.
Under the mass, I keep a slip of plastic sheeting,
punched to let the liquid seep toward the rhubarb.
In March, I fish the rope out the back,
drag the frozen ark, draped in ripped sails,
down through the raspberries to the woods.
I stash it there between the rocks.
Wild animals tiptoe around it, but insects
build their city.

I hide the load far from my dogs. They will, if they can,
return me to myself, the vacations of my friends
into the kitchen . . . a communal smear,
sachet behind the ear, on their shoulders
the luxury so regularly voided.
I can tell a dog that has been rolling in shit
by the smile it wears
crossing the lawn toward me like a fundamentalist.

THE TENT CATERPILLERS

The wild cherries are hung with nurses' panty hose.
We try to burn them out, immolate these nuns, these aerial
gypsies, these merchants in their peaked hats and sheets.
High up, the big bags, dirigible, tense with overpopulation,
send out live chains, freights along the branches to Dachau.
Torched, they drop, smoking like spent rockets.
In the morning, they still go back and forth to the ruins.

The nests go gray and seedy. We check our collars,
rake our hair. The sound of chewing is the afternoon.
They punctuate the windshield, exclamations and questions,
carpeting the driveway. We watch our step. With shards
we cut them in half. The bile surges like oil.
We hate these Arabs, tucking their cocoons in the corners
of the porch, the garage. Investing in our soil.
There isn't a bird, no rodent will eat them. Our women
grow confused, scream at the children, then praise
the slaughter all over the sidewalk. The men go out with Raid
House and Garden Bug Spray to gas the japonicas, the plum trees
and all the roses. Tiny body bags shrivel on their half leaves.
But thousands more are coming. Their clothes look expensive.
Mink and camel hair, they select our pink, our white flowering,
our green and fruitful. They crawl our way, obsequious and poor.
They have fuzzy ideas, make stalled remarks, but are ambitious.
We fog the whole damned jungle. They fall like snipers.
We sweep them into piles, pour on the gasoline and burn Miami,
Woodstock, Teheran, the boat people, all of Havana.

We go inside, exhausted. We close the windows,
blessing the screens. We check our children,
asleep in the air-conditioned rooms, draw the gauzy sheers,
wish the yard, the street, the trees all white with snow.

FOCUS

Bent to berries in the field,
she peers beneath the pines to see the trilium,
the Indian Pipe, bled some millennia, that work
from bleached seed, spores left winter-long
like satellites in ice. It is a bronze day. Her bucket fills.
Drained of mind, on a dead-end road, she seldom remembers
the river sliding by, the tide crawling the mud
where bright gulls paddle behind the house.

These shaded flowers are her favorites. She raises none.
The front yard is carpeted with wood chips, maple
that smells like cheap wine steaming in the sun.
On the line, one pair of small thermal underwear, hung since spring
and grayer than her skin. Her son's.
At the high-water mark, behind a rock, he hides with his .22
then cracks the bell of the afternoon. A flower explodes,
mauls itself black at the water's edge.

Over the river, Chas. O. Welch, 90, bolts in his chair,
cocks his head, sure again he heard something.
A woman is running in the field . . . his first wife,
legs flashing, chasing the pig they ate in 1914,
the white Poland China he finally cornered,
nailed with a shot
exactly where the eyes and the ears cross.

SONNET

The stones do not heat every day, but give up
a little gray, polite radiance before they vanish under snow.
This evening, collar up, stomach full, I am impressed
by stolid accomplishment, as I sidle the wall,
scuffling leaves. I've summered well, admiring things.
This wall may be the one that belts the earth seven times,
beginning here. There's Hadrian, riding his horse,
up and down, up and down, depressed,
on one side of everything he's mastered.

I do not eat every day.
All the way back to the house,
I treat myself to what is left,
the kindly, senile humor of the stones.
A strange place warms me more.

ENDANGERED SPECIES

Through dawn, night dwindles toward me,
as if I were drawing it into the blind,
my net, my worth. The sun rounds the granite head,
pinks the ice-caked marsh, then sheds a little light on me,
who listens for blessings, the cold, holy gossip of ducks.

It might be like this to be dying on an arctic mission,
rapt but exhausted on the sled, trapped inside an igloo
with an intuition of the light, of what it would be like
to bring down angels with a blast, their bodies
gorgeously feathered, chevrons of torched steel
at the ailerons. My god, just to walk back into this life
hot with evidence!

My knees are crystal, my fingers tuning forks.
I rise to go. It is an average day, sunny and cold.
Suddenly, a marsh hawk, fanning like a brush fire,
breaks its dive. The lean head, beak, the spread talons
stretch for the decoy, while the wings beat and lift,
lift the animal and glide away,
a glide so sad I sit.

I tricked it. Up close, the glory,
but did not shoot.
Dazed, I stagger through the pasture,
in the kitchen hang my gun.
I sweat, my hair as wet as a baby's.
I am saved for the wrong world.

MEDITATION

Forking cowshit behind the barn. No deader,
more gratifying weight at the end of a handle.
At the other end, my body. Stressed beyond pain,
my arms swing like rockers, my knees pop and carp,
boots sinking in the mire. I think about simplicity,
solitude and sinking. Work like this is grand,
my own red ocean in my ears, like vacuuming a house,
anonymous within the roar, looking outward
into the dark audience, a star in the universal opera.
From the streamered window, the calf blats.

Poor, dumb beast. It hasn't my nostalgia for the future,
the quiet stretch, primeval and thoughtless
as the dung pile itself, a heraldry
where thumb-sized slugs drag beneath the squash leaves
like wounded retainers, where grubs curl,
white as canonical hats, appliquéd with gold and crimson.
Shit will not adhere to their bodies.
They are immortal, as are the irridescent beetles
wandering in armor, battle-dazed and aimless,
that claw the flakes and clods for God knows what.
The worms, too, immaculate, dart and pull,
skewering the ruins. I stare at the calf, like me,
crapped and plastered.

An angel of sorts has blown its horn.
Now I can be stupid by the gate, waving when you come.
I may blat back to reassure you. Touched,
I might tender you, lick the sweat from your arm,
nuzzle your groin, display that other adoration, ladylike,
for any clean-shaved farmer, younger than I am,
who walks toward me with an intelligent grin,
a pail full of apples and grain, a rifle and knife.

BY A RIVER IN SOUTHERN OHIO

Steam rises from the surface in ghost-smokes.
The bourbon slows with cold. A heron is rigid,
a scientist picking along the bank.
A carp rolls, long as a brown boy studying the bottom,
nosing the paper drapery,
blinking at the flash of disposables among the rocks,
green with baby hair.

The air will freeze and be bright all day.
We will hustle from sun to shade and back,
see small birds walk upon the bordering skim
like ornaments reflected in a ghetto window, behind which
denizens starve and sleep, their brains seized,
their eyes cast in bronze.

Given light, these shun the nuance,
so fundamental is their need.
All the big rivers, every tributary, contain them,
mouthing their muddy thoughts and wild bibles.
It is a sin to net or spear them, so primitive a species.
They may be baited, hooked with tinsel lures, but,
beached, they gape and gasp as if to speak.
We throw them back. They are not good to eat.

FOLLOWING FISH

In what is left of a tide, the vast memory,
you slog a little Mississippi
that cuts the marsh into a two-piece puzzle.
You have traveled for eons, in hip boots,
heavy with a body you've outgrown.
The fish zips in the riffles like blue-water thought.
It turns to skirt you, but you block it with your feet,
its instinct clearer than your own.

You see what the fish sees always,
the engram printed on its circuits, the silhouetted
osprey, holding on the air.
You have feelings in the matter: fear, cruelty,
greed and pain. You interfere with the ideal
by being there.

So you stay until the water rises.
No, shoo the fish to deeper water.
Or step aside, watch it dart downstream
below the bird that drifts and hovers
before it drops.

In Maine, when summer folk are gone, inland,
animals come from the woods.
Coon sort compost. Ravens pick the gardens.
Fox snap groundmoles before frost.
In the ditch near a battered blackberry patch,
the seedy, purple cylinders of bear.

I remember how flakes sailed once like Easter gloves.
Roadside, beyond the sluggish wipers, a three-legged
coyote, feeding off the concrete, hopped through the fence,
looked back as if it were a dog.

Tonight, there are no limits in the dark,
west or out to sea. We have faith in trees,
memory healed within the bark. An animal
steps toward us through the leaves.

THE TAME GRIEVE

The owl gathers light,
the glint from a shrew's ebony toenail.
It can discern the candle from the flame
two miles away, and deer, grinding cedar tips,
stop to watch a sudden conformation of stumps,
hunching in the leaves, or pick out a rabbit's blink,
a key that snicks in the ignition.

The tame grieve.
The bone-white cow by the gate
gazes past the horse that sleepwalks into the pasture,
where the cat, slit-eyed on a rick, pities Asia.
They mourn whole valleys, simple vistas,
given a wide outlook and a place to park.

Below the golden scum of pollen on the pond,
well after our deaths, the beautiful young pickerel
vees to deeper water when a shadow comes,
or shivers forward toward the shiny, fitful darter,
any wounded we'd have sung.

THE MAN DOWN THE ROAD

From my post against this rock,
one load chambered, the other in my pocket,
I have simply pulped the hearts of several deer.
His go down akimbo in a semiautomatic blast,
jumped from their beds like peasants.
Mine drop to their knees.
I am this thoughtful.

He is younger than I am.
His kids in red sweaters blaze in the yard.
His wife, empty this spring, rakes debris.
In his fatigues, he yawns and stretches on the porch.
I usually see him, though, bent beneath the pines, tracking.
He is the animal I watch for in myself.
I DO NOT MOVE.
He is too dangerous.

ABOUT THE AUTHOR

Paul Nelson was born in 1934, near Boston, of parents who had emigrated from Norway and Finland when children and who are retired now on the coast of Maine not far from where the poet and his painter wife, Judith, live on their old farm in Machiasport. His grandfathers were fishermen and stonecutters, one on Vinalhaven, the other in Quincy. As he grew up, his parents moved many times, mostly within New England but also to the Bronx, New Jersey, and Chicago, as he himself has moved from job to job in Hawaii, upstate New York, Vermont, Indiana, Colorado, and Ohio. Transience and commitment to place and belief are subjects of his poetry. He says, "I have no accent."

Nelson was educated at Dartmouth and Colgate, working in Medieval and Renaissance studies in English, with emphasis on seventeenth-century poetry. He has taught, particularly at Goddard College, where he chaired the Literature and Writing faculty for several years, courses ranging from Greek drama and myth to contemporary fiction and poetry.

In 1978–79 Nelson was awarded an NEA fellowship for poems now in *Days Off*. His other books include *Cargo* (1972), *Ice* (1974), and *Average Nights* (1977). He writes occasional reviews and teaches for the Creative Writing Program at Ohio University.

ABOUT THE SERIES

Since 1975, Virginia Commonwealth University has sponsored publication of the winning manuscript in the annual AWP Award Series in Poetry, an open competition for book-length manuscripts. Established in 1974 in a cooperative arrangement between VCU and the University Press of Virginia, the award carries a $1,000 honorarium and an invitation for the winning author to read at the AWP Annual Meeting.

Manuscripts are received by the series director, who divides them among readers, who are published poets. Finalists are selected and the manuscripts are submitted to a final judge who chooses the winning book. Final judges for the series have included Richard Eberhart, Elizabeth Bishop, Robert Penn Warren, Donald Justice, and Maxine Kumin. William Meredith chose *Days Off* as the first-place selection in the 1981 AWP Award Series.

For further information and guidelines for submission write: The Associated Writing Programs, Old Dominion University, Norfolk, Virginia 23508.

THE VIRGINIA COMMONWEALTH UNIVERSITY SERIES

FOR CONTEMPORARY POETRY   WALTON BEACHAM, GENERAL EDITOR

Moving Out
    by David Walker   1976

The Ventriloquist
    by Robert Huff   1977

Rites of Strangers
    by Phyllis Janowitz   1978

James Cook in Search of Terra Incognita
    by Jeanne Larsen   1979

Following Gravity
    by James Applewhite   1980

The Hours of Morning
    by William Carpenter   1981